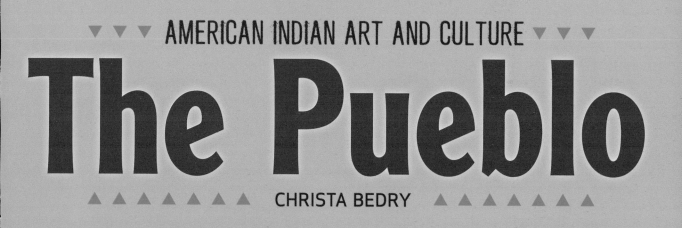

AMERICAN INDIAN ART AND CULTURE

The Pueblo

CHRISTA BEDRY

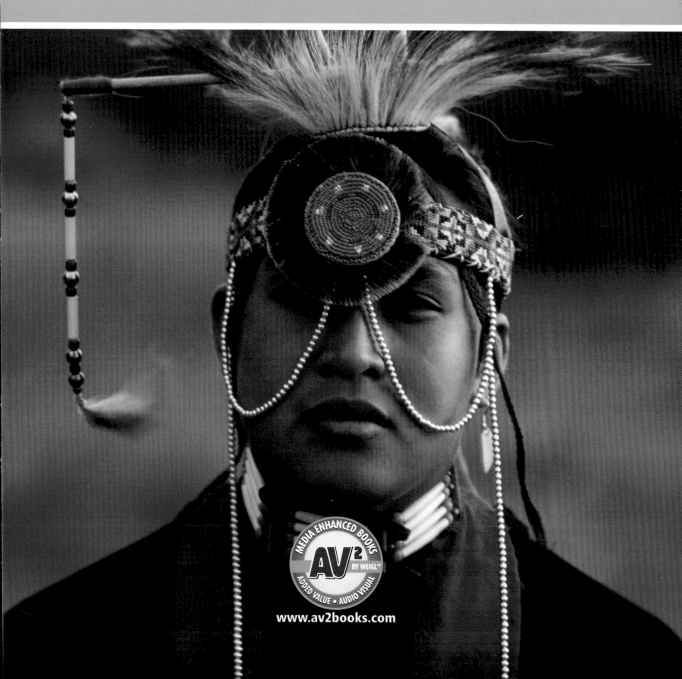

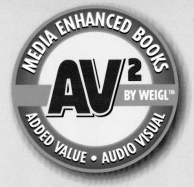

AV² provides enriched content that supplements and complements this book. Weigl's AV² books strive to create inspired learning and engage young minds in a total learning experience.

Your AV² Media Enhanced books come alive with...

Audio
Listen to sections of the book read aloud.

Key Words
Study vocabulary, and complete a matching word activity.

Video
Watch informative video clips.

Quizzes
Test your knowledge.

Embedded Weblinks
Gain additional information for research.

Slide Show
View images and captions, and prepare a presentation.

Go to **www.av2books.com**, and enter this book's unique code.

BOOK CODE

U 5 9 6 5 3 9

Try This!
Complete activities and hands-on experiments.

AV² by Weigl brings you media enhanced books that support active learning.

... and much, much more!

Published by AV² by Weigl
350 5th Avenue, 59th Floor
New York, NY 10118

Websites: www.av2books.com   www.weigl.com

Library of Congress Cataloging-in-Publication Data
Bedry, Christa.
 The Pueblo / Christa Bedry.
    pages cm. -- (American Indian art and culture)
Originally published: 2004.
Includes bibliographical references and index.
 ISBN 978-1-4896-2922-7 (hard cover : alk. paper) -- ISBN 978-1-4896-2923-4 (soft cover : alk. paper) -- ISBN 978-1-4896-2924-1 (single user ebook) -- ISBN 978-1-4896-2925-8 (multi-user ebook)
 1. Pueblo Indians--History--Juvenile literature. 2. Pueblo Indians--Social life and customs--Juvenile literature. I. Title.
 E99.P9B379 2014
 978.9004'974--dc23
                                    2014038980

Printed in the United States of America in Brainerd, Minnesota
1 2 3 4 5 6 7 8 9 18 17 16 15 14

122014
WEP051214

Project Coordinator: Heather Kissock
Art Director: Terry Paulhus

Every reasonable effort has been made to trace ownership and to obtain permission to reprint copyright material. The publishers would be pleased to have any errors or omissions brought to their attention so that they may be corrected in subsequent printings.

Weigl acknowledges Getty Images, iStock, and Alamy as its primary image suppliers for this title.

Contents

The People

More than 1,000 years ago, a group of American Indians called the Pueblo peoples lived in small villages made of stone and mud in northwestern New Mexico and northeastern Arizona. They belonged to four separate language groups called **dialects**, but their way of life was quite similar. This is because they shared the same history. Their **ancestors**, the Ancestral **Puebloans**, or Anasazi, settled and farmed in the Four Corners region of the Southwest between about A.D. 1 and A.D. 1300.

In 1540, Spanish explorer Francisco Vasquez de Coronado traveled through the American southwest. He called the people who lived in permanent towns "Pueblos" after their unusual **adobe** dwellings. Pueblo means "town" in the Spanish language. It also refers to a single adobe house.

PUEBLO MAP

Location of Pueblo villages in New Mexico

0   50 Miles

50 Kilometers

Legend
- Pueblo Villages
- City

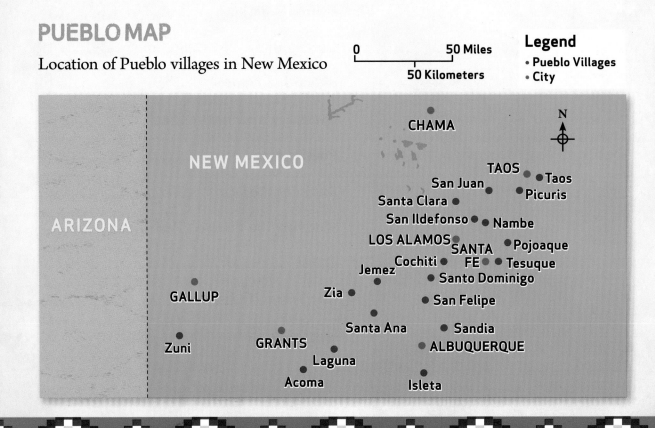

ARIZONA

NEW MEXICO

CHAMA

N

TAOS   Taos

San Juan   Picuris

Santa Clara

San Ildefonso   Nambe

LOS ALAMOS   SANTA   Pojoaque

Cochiti   FE   Tesuque

Jemez   Santo Dominigo

GALLUP   Zia

San Felipe

Santa Ana   Sandia

Zuni   GRANTS   ALBUQUERQUE

Laguna

Acoma   Isleta

Long ago, the Pueblo peoples' livelihood depended on farming and trading in western and central New Mexico, eastern Arizona, and western Texas. They built pueblos along the rocky edges of canyons. This allowed them to save the nearby farmland for their crops. It also enabled them to stay close to the rivers running through the canyon below.

Today, most Pueblo peoples live in cities. Others live in the few remaining pueblos along the Rio Grande River in New Mexico. The Western Pueblos include Hopi and Zuni peoples. Hopi peoples live on three **mesas** in northeast Arizona. The Zuni peoples live in a very large pueblo in western New Mexico.

Traditionally, Puebloans who have left their villages make return visits in order to carry on their cultural traditions.

AMERICA'S FIRST FARMERS

The Pueblo were some of America's first farmers. Their most important crops were corn, beans, and squash. These plants are known as the **"three sisters."**

Men cleared the fields and prepared the soil for **farming**.

Women did the rest of the **farm work**, such as **planting crops, weeding, watering,** and **harvesting**.

The Pueblo developed **farming** techniques to hold water in the dry soil.

The Pueblo traded local goods such as CORN for TURQUOISE, SALT, SEASHELLS, and COLORFUL MACAW FEATHERS from as far away as Mexico and the coast of California.

Pueblo Homes

Imagine living in a house that is 100 years old. Today, some Pueblo peoples live in much older homes. Their pueblo dwellings look much like the homes their ancestors built hundreds of years ago.

Pueblo houses look like apartments, which are stacked on top of one another like a staircase. Each family's house consists of a few connected rooms. In the past, people entered pueblos through a trapdoor in the roof. They used ladders to get to the roof. Today, pueblos have hinged doors and glass windows, which face toward a central **plaza**. Some very large pueblos have more than one plaza.

The thick stone walls of a pueblo provide excellent insulation. Pueblos are warm in winter and cool in summer.

The walls of pueblo homes are made from stones or blocks that are covered with adobe mud. The inner walls of pueblos are covered with a layer of white mud called **gypsum**. This keeps the home clean and bright.

In the past, Pueblo ancestors used ladders to get from one level of a pueblo to another. Ladders are still used in this way today

DWELLING AND DECORATION

Traditionally, pueblo homes had thick, flat roofs. Pueblo peoples placed large logs called vigas across the top of their houses to support the flat roofs. Flat roofs provided an extra space where people could visit or work.

The Pueblo peoples took vigas from nearby mountain forests and hauled them to the desert. The ends of the logs usually pointed beyond the top ledges of the house, through the adobe wall. Vigas were covered with small sticks, grass mats, and mud.

Pueblo Communities

In many ways, the Pueblo peoples' lifestyle has not changed much over the years. They still follow many of their cultural traditions. However, modern life has had an effect on the Pueblo peoples. Changes in transportation, work methods, tools, and other recent conveniences have made their way into Pueblo life. Although many villagers now work beyond Pueblo land, most still practice the traditions of their ancestors, including ceremonies and art.

Traditionally, the Pueblo peoples had to cooperate to survive in their dry environment. They worked together and performed jobs according to a schedule. If one family's crops failed, neighbors and family members offered help. Men wove cloth and baskets, built houses, and led ceremonies. Women prepared food, cared for the children, made pottery, and transported water. They also helped the men build houses and weave baskets and clothing. Pueblo children worked in the fields.

Each village had its own government and land area. The town government had a **council**, which was ruled by an elected chief. Pueblo priests were community leaders. They were responsible for handing out medicine to villagers. They also decided when the village would go to war or hunt.

New Mexico's Taos Pueblo is the largest multi-storied Pueblo structure in the United States. There has been a strong community living in the Taos Pueblo for more than 1,000 years.

CHILDREN

Pueblo boys played darts. The darts were **pointed sticks**, with **feathers** on one end, stuck through **corncobs**.

Pueblo families shared their belongings. **Children** did not have their own **possessions**.

Children often played a game with **pa-tol** sticks. They threw the sticks into a circle of rocks and tried to hit the **stone** in the **middle**.

Pueblo babies wore "diapers" made from **pounded juniper bark**.

Pueblo Clothing

Long ago, most Pueblo peoples made their clothes from woven cloth rather than the animal hides other American Indian nations used. Some communities in colder areas used animal hides for clothing. Their ancestors, the Ancestral Puebloans, had been growing, spinning, dying, and weaving cotton since at least A.D. 800. When the Spanish settlers arrived and brought sheep, the Puebloans began spinning sheep's wool into yarn to make clothing.

Men and boys wore shirts, along with loose pants or short skirts. Women and girls wore blankets called **mantas**, which had one strap over the right shoulder. They wore colorful dresses or long sleeved shirts beneath the mantas.

In the winter, the Pueblo peoples draped warm, woven blankets around themselves.

In the warm summer months, Pueblo peoples did not wear many clothes. Men wore a breechcloth, which was a piece of leather or cloth tied around their waist. Women wore cotton or wool dresses. The Puebloans also wove colorful sashes. These long strips of cloth could be tied as belts to hold the blankets in place.

In the past, Puebloan men and women often decorated themselves with jewelry. Today, many Pueblo still make jewelry from turquoise, **obsidian**, shells, coral, and silver. Each pueblo has its own style of jewelry making.

ADORNMENTS

Long ago, Puebloans went barefoot. Beginning in A.D. 500 to 700, they wove sandals made from the **yucca** plant and moccasins of deerskin. The moccasins worn by the Pueblo peoples were unique. Most nations wore low moccasins around the foot. The Puebloans wore high ones that went up the calf. Men wore their moccasins above the ankle. Women wore their moccasins slightly below the knee. They wrapped white deerskin around their legs up to their knees. The hard soles of all moccasins were bent slightly up and over the side of the foot.

Pueblo Food

For hundreds of years, the Pueblo peoples have had a wide and varied diet. Ancestral Puebloans tamed turkeys and raised them for meat and eggs. Sometimes, they hunted antelope, birds, deer, elks, prairie dogs, and rabbits. Spanish settlers introduced the Pueblo peoples to fruits, chilies, onions, and tomatoes.

Corn was one of the Pueblo peoples' staple foods. Pueblo women ground up the corn and made it into flat breads called tortillas. They cooked tortillas and other foods in a *horno*. These dome-shaped ovens were built by covering bricks with mud.

Corn came in many varieties and colors. Farmers often passed their own special corn varieties down to their sons.

Blue corn, which grows on smaller cobs than yellow corn, has been an important crop to the Pueblo for hundreds of years.

Traditional horno ovens are still used today.

Blue Corn Tortillas

Ingredients:

- 1/3 cup flour
- 1 cup water
- 1-2/3 cup blue or yellow cornmeal

Equipment:

- large bowl
- wax paper
- pan
- spatula
- rolling pin

Directions

1. Stir all the ingredients together in a large bowl.

2. Make 12 dough balls. Flatten the balls into tortillas by rolling each ball between two sheets of greased wax paper. You can also pat the ball between your hands until it is a thin tortilla.

3. Cook the tortilla in a lightly greased pan. Heat each side until it is a light brown color.

4. Remove from heat, let cool, and enjoy.

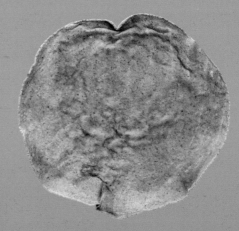

Tools, Weapons, and Defense

The Pueblo peoples used tools to make their tasks easier. Pueblo women used tools for grinding corn. A Pueblo woman cut dried corn kernels off the cob. She placed the corn kernels on a *matate*, a large, flat stone that had a dent in the center. A smaller stone called a *mano* was rolled over the matate to grind the corn. After the kernels were ground once, they were moved to smoother stones, and the process was repeated.

To farm in their fields, the Pueblo peoples used wooden digging sticks. They used hoes made from stone or animal bone to clear the land. Today, the Pueblo peoples use modern farming equipment.

The Pueblo peoples also created special tools for making pottery or weaving baskets and clothes. They used upright **looms** and wooden spindle whorls for weaving. A spindle is a wooden rod that is used to twist fibers into thread. The whorl is used to keep the spinning wheel moving at a regular speed.

The Ancestral Puebloans were the first American Indians to weave on upright looms.

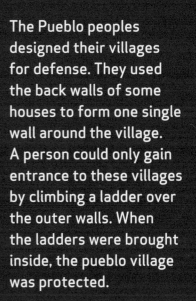

Before Spanish settlers arrived in North America, the Pueblo peoples used bows and arrows to hunt. Arrowheads and knives were made from rocks. Pueblo men flaked or shaped the rocks to make them sharp. Other weapons included the **lance**, club, and shield. Beautiful shields are still used during ceremonies.

The Pueblo peoples designed their villages for defense. They used the back walls of some houses to form one single wall around the village. A person could only gain entrance to these villages by climbing a ladder over the outer walls. When the ladders were brought inside, the pueblo village was protected.

The Zuni and Hopi defended themselves by building their villages on high mesas. It was hard for invaders to climb the steep sides of the mesas.

Pueblo Religion

The Pueblo respected nature and treated each other with kindness. They were truthful and respectful of their parents and seniors. Every part of Puebloan life was based on spirituality. As part of every activity, from planting, to building, to hunting, to chores, Pueblo peoples prayed and made offerings. They often used cornmeal as an offering to the spirits.

When the Spanish settlers arrived, they punished the Puebloans who would not change their beliefs and become Christians. This forced Puebloans to practice their religion secretly. They believed that religion was a way to create **harmony** with the universe. However, the Pueblo peoples knew becoming Christian would help establish harmony with the settlers. As a result, they were willing to add the new religion to their own religious beliefs. Some of the Christian saints were included in the **kachinas**. Today, many Pueblo peoples are Christians, but still maintain some of their ancient beliefs.

The San Francisco de Assisi Mission Church in Ranchos de Taos, New Mexico, shows the blending of Pueblo and Christian cultures. The church is built using pueblo adobe construction, but its design follows that of traditional Christian churches.

The Pueblo made dolls to represent the various kachinas. Each kachina was represented by specific colors and materials.

KACHINAS

Kachinas have particular **powers**. Some can **bring rain**. Others offer **healing** or **protection**.

Traditionally, kachina dolls are carved by men and given to girls at ceremonies in the spring and summer.

Parents often hang the dolls above their babies' cradles.

Kachinas have humanlike relationships. This includes getting married and having children.

The **kachina dolls** are used to **teach about** the **300 different** kachina **spirits** they represent.

The dolls are **carved by hand** out of **cottonwood root.** They are painted and sometimes decorated with **feathers, fur, shells, leather,** and **yarn.**

Ceremonies and Celebrations

The Puebloans held important ceremonies throughout the year. Some ceremonies were based on Pueblo religion. Other ceremonies combined ancient southwestern traditions with Christian celebrations. During ceremonies, the Puebloans performed complex dances. Each dance used specific movements to tell a story about an act of nature.

For example, the Pueblo peoples performed a ceremony at each stage of the farming season. There were dances and ceremonies before planting. Once the crops were planted, there were other dances and ceremonies to bring rain and protect the crops. The biggest celebration came with the harvest of the crops. The Pueblo peoples performed the Corn Dance after the harvest. This was a dance of thanksgiving for the crop and a prayer for rain during the next farming season. The Puebloans also held ceremonies following a successful hunt or to celebrate wisdom and strength.

The Matachines dance mixes Pueblo and Spanish Christian traditions. It is a religious dance that tells the story of the Spanish invasion of Central and South America.

KIVAS

Many religious ceremonies were carried out in round rooms called kivas. The kivas were built underground, so they would be warm in the winter and cool in the summer. The walls of the kivas were decorated with paintings of Kokopelli and other important gods. Every member of a Pueblo village belonged to a kiva society. Pueblo women built the kivas, but only men were allowed inside. Each society was responsible for specific ceremonies.

Music and Dance

Music is an important part of Pueblo life. Children use small drums to learn traditional songs. Drums are made by stretching rawhide across the top of hollowed cottonwood branches. Pueblo children also shake rattles, which are made by filling **gourds** with dried beans.

Traditional Pueblo dances vary from one pueblo village to another. For the most part, dances are part of religious ceremonies performed to ask the gods for rain and good crops.

During the Eagle Dance, Pueblo dancers dress up as eagles. They wear feather armbands and white caps with yellow bills. The dancers make flying movements. This dance is performed because some Pueblo peoples believe the eagle can bring rain by talking to the gods who live above the clouds.

The herrera drum is a traditional Pueblo instrument. Hide is used to cover the drum, which has handles mounted to the wooden drum body.

CEREMONIAL DANCING

The Eagle Dance is often associated with curing illness.

The Snake Dance is one of the Hopi's best-known dances. The Hopi believe there are gods who live under the ground. They believe snakes talk to these gods. The snakes ask the gods to provide enough water for the Hopi peoples. As part of the dance to the gods, dancers dress up in red cloths that are painted with a black zigzag pattern. This pattern represents the snakes. Other patterns show footprints of water creatures such as ducks and frogs. During one part of the dance, each dancer carries a live snake in his mouth.

One of the most important Zuni dances is the Shalako dance. During this dance, men wear costumes that represent the gods. The men dance throughout the night in new homes that were built for them in the Zuni village. The following day, they have a race to plant prayer sticks in the ground. Prayer sticks are made from willow that is found by the river. The prayer sticks are carved, painted, and decorated with feathers. The sticks help bring health and **fertility** to the village's crops, people, and animals.

The Hopi peoples believed that snakes were their brothers and could be relied on to take their messages to the underworld, where the rain gods lived.

Language and Storytelling

The Pueblo peoples spoke four languages. The languages were Hopi, Zuni, Keres, and Tano. Over time, they developed into six languages—Hopi, Zuni, Keresan, Tiwa, Towa, and Tewa. Tiwa, Towa, and Tewa are dialects of the Tano language. The Zuni language is not spoken in any other region. It is a distinct language. Today, Pueblo peoples also speak English, and many speak Spanish, too.

The Pueblo peoples enjoyed telling stories for entertainment as well as to teach lessons about the past. To help tell these stories, they made dolls, which represented the characters. The coyote was a popular figure in their stories.

Storyteller dolls are a modern Pueblo tradition. They represent tribal elders telling stories to Pueblo children.

Each pueblo community has its own myth to explain such mysteries as the creation of Earth. As a result, creation stories differ from one pueblo to another. However, they have some common features. For example, Sun Father, Moon Mother, and the creation of the first people on Earth are common to all Pueblo creation stories.

The coyote is often portrayed as a trickster in Pueblo stories. His misadventures are meant to teach Pueblo children valuable life lessons.

KOKOPELLI

One of the most important figures in Pueblo myths or legends is the god Kokopelli. Drawings of Kokopelli appear on caves, pottery, and inside kiva walls. Traditions vary between pueblos, but Kokopelli is usually shown as a humpbacked man with a flute.

By performing ceremonies, the Pueblo were asking Kokopelli to bring rain and good crops. Some people believed that Kokopelli would bring fertility to humans and livestock. Kokopelli used his flute to talk to the gods and ask for the things people wanted. He used the hump on his back to bring gifts to the world.

🏚 Pueblo Art

The Pueblo are well known for their pottery, baskets, jewelry, and blankets. Each Pueblo community uses unique patterns in their pottery, baskets, and weaving.

Traditionally, the Pueblo peoples used a coil method to make pottery. This artistic tradition continues today. Potters roll clay into long, narrow coils. They place the coils on top of one another to form a pot. Then, potters smooth the coils to make a flat surface. They paint designs or carve patterns on the pot. Finally, they fire the pots. Traditionally, the Pueblo fired pots in outdoor pits. Today, they fire pots in electric kilns.

The Pueblo used various plants to make baskets. The different colors of these plants produced many patterns. Basket makers still use a traditional method to make baskets. The basket maker begins by joining several pieces of **cattail**, which have been soaked in water.

There are many different designs used in Pueblo pottery. Black geometric designs on a cream background are popular in the Santo Domingo style.

The cattails are wrapped with willow and twisted into a coil on the bottom of the basket. An **awl** is used to pierce holes and pull willow around the cattail coil. This pattern continues as the basket maker builds the sides of the basket.

Pueblo men and women have been weaving since about A.D. 800. The Ancestral Puebloans, or Anasazi, used plant fibers, such as cotton and yucca, to weave. They wove bags, belts, blankets, clothing, footwear, and hats. Later, they began to weave with wool. The Pueblo peoples invented the upright weaving looms. Sometimes, the Pueblo include weaving as part of religious ceremonies.

Large baskets were made to store grain and vegetables.

ART FORMS

By **1840**, about **20,000** Pueblo **woven** blankets were being exported to **Mexico** every year.

Boiled **wild spinach** is used to make **pottery** that is **black in color.**

Rocks and **clay** are used to make the colors **red**, **white**, and **yellow** in **pottery.**

In the past, **Pueblo artists** used **yucca leaf brushes** to create **rock art** and to **paint** on **pottery.**

Pueblo **pottery** was usually **made by women** and **decorated by men.**

Zuni Fetishes

The Zuni peoples believed that, during the creation of the world, the Sun God's twin sons used lightning to turn animals into stones. The Zuni believed the animals' spirits were kept alive inside these stones. They thought the stones had special powers that could be used to protect the Zuni from other animals. The Zuni peoples believed that each stone maintained the characteristics of the animal it resembled. People hunted for stones that looked like animals.

Bear fetishes are used for healing, protection, strength, traveling, mothering, hunting, and gathering.

They had the stones blessed by a **medicine man**. These blessed animal-shaped stones were called fetishes. Zuni peoples also carved fetishes out of hard items, such as stones and shells.

Fetishes were believed to bring luck, power, and protection. Zuni peoples used fetishes for healing and hunting, as well as for spiritual and ceremonial reasons. Fetishes have become an important art form in the Zuni community. About 400 Zuni artists still make fetishes. A favorite saying taught to all Zuni children is "take care of the fetish and it will take care of you."

The turtle has always been highly regarded as it carries its home on its back. The turtle fetish is a reminder to respect Mother Earth.

STUDYING THE PUEBLO'S PAST

Archaeologists study items left by cultures from the past. Pueblo peoples from the past left many items behind. Archaeologists have been able to study these items to learn more about the Pueblo peoples.

Archaeologists have also explored the ancient ruins of Pueblo villages. They have found proof that the Anasazi were the ancestors of today's modern Pueblo people. These Ancestral Puebloans lived in the area between 100 B.C. and A.D. 1300. They lived in caves or built shelters using wood poles and adobe mud. The Anasazi hunted animals for food, gathered wild plants, and grew squash and corn. They wove baskets and made pottery.

By studying building ruins, archaeologists can learn about the history and development of a people.

Timeline

Paleo-Indian and Archaic Period

Pre-10,000—B.C 1500.

Pueblo ancestors hunted animals and gathered wild plants. They used natural shelters and made temporary structures. They wove some items. They moved with the changing seasons.

Basketmaker

1500 B.C.—A.D. 750

Pueblo ancestors built permanent houses and started farming. They wove sandals and baskets and began making pottery.

Pueblo I and I I Period

750 A.D.—1150

The Anasazi began building large villages from wood and adobe. From 900, stone construction was used. Ceremonial chambers developed into the kiva. The Pueblo made pottery of many shapes and styles.

The Pueblo peoples used to shape stone into blocks. They would build large villages with four or five layers of houses. Each village had its own method of putting the rocks and mud together. On some very old houses, archaeologists have found the fingerprints of the people who smeared the adobe mud on the walls.

Mesa Verde National Park in Colorado is the largest archaeological reserve in the United States. It is home to more than 4,000 archaeological sites and more than 600 Pueblo cliff dwellings.

Pueblo III Period

1150 A.D.—1300

The Anasazi spread into central Utah, southern California, and northern Mexico.

Pueblo IV Period

1300 A.D.—1600

The Pueblo developed large villages of plaza-type pueblos. Pottery became less detailed.

Pueblo V Period

1600—present

The Pueblo began raising animals. Agriculture replaced gathering. Wool replaced cotton for cloth. Handicrafts and tourism provided income. Many people moved into modern homes near their traditional pueblos.

QUIZ

1 What does the word "pueblo" mean in the Spanish language?

A. Town

2 What are pueblo houses made of?

A. Stones or blocks covered with adobe mud

3 What were the main crops grown by the Pueblo peoples?

A. Beans, corn, and squash

4 What tool did the Pueblo create for weaving cloth?

A. Upright loom

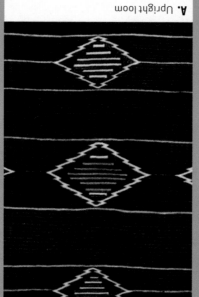

5 Who did most of the farming in traditional Pueblo communities?

A. Women

6 What kinds of dolls are given to Pueblo children to teach them about the spirits?

A. Kachina dolls

7 Who is one of the most important figures in Pueblo myths and legends?

A. Kokopelli

8 When did the Pueblo peoples begin weaving?

A. About A.D. 800

9 What are carved stones that look like animals called?

A. Fetishes

10 When did Pueblo ancestors start building permanent houses and take up farming?

A. 1500 B.C.—A.D. 750

KEY WORDS

adobe: red mud that is used to make bricks

ancestors: relatives who lived a very long time ago

archaeologists: scientists who study objects from the past to learn about people who lived long ago

awl: a sharp tool used for making holes in soft materials

cattail: a tall rush with long, flat leaves and flowers

council: a group of leaders who give advice and make decisions for the entire community

dialects: variations on a language that is spoken in a certain place

fertility: the ability to have many children or for a field to grow much food

gourds: vegetables that have a hard skin and can be hollowed out

gypsum: a mineral used to make plaster products

harmony: getting along with one's surroundings

kachinas: ancestral spirits of the Pueblo peoples

lance: a long, wooden spear

looms: wooden frames that are used for weaving

mantas: blankets with one strap over the right shoulder

medicine man: someone who has the power to cure illnesses and can communicate with spirits

mesas: flat-topped pieces of land that are high above the rest of the land

obsidian: a kind of glassy black volcanic stone

plaza: a central area in a village, which is used for gathering, working, and playing

Puebloans: Pueblo peoples

yucca: a low shrub that can be used for cloth fibers, sharp needles, and paint brushes

INDEX

Log on to www.av2books.com

AV² by Weigl brings you media enhanced books that support active learning. Go to www.av2books.com, and enter the special code found on page 2 of this book. You will gain access to enriched and enhanced content that supplements and complements this book. Content includes video, audio, weblinks, quizzes, a slide show, and activities.

AV² Online Navigation

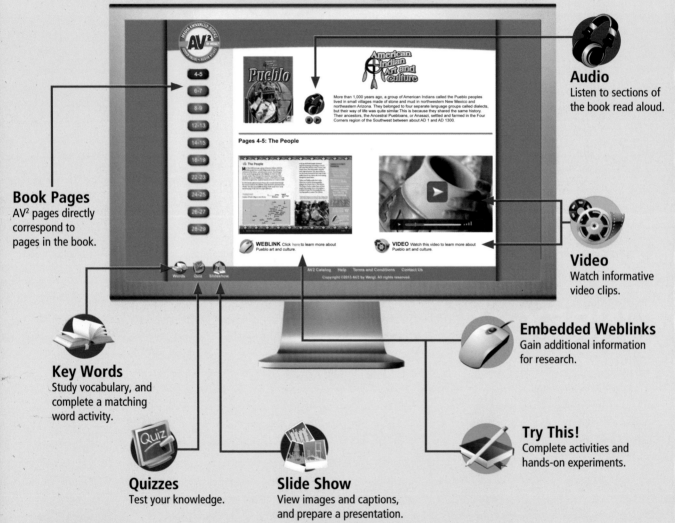

Book Pages
AV² pages directly correspond to pages in the book.

Key Words
Study vocabulary, and complete a matching word activity.

Quizzes
Test your knowledge.

Slide Show
View images and captions, and prepare a presentation.

Audio
Listen to sections of the book read aloud.

Video
Watch informative video clips.

Embedded Weblinks
Gain additional information for research.

Try This!
Complete activities and hands-on experiments.

AV² was built to bridge the gap between print and digital. We encourage you to tell us what you like and what you want to see in the future.

Sign up to be an AV² Ambassador at www.av2books.com/ambassador.

Due to the dynamic nature of the Internet, some of the URLs and activities provided as part of AV² by Weigl may have changed or ceased to exist. AV² by Weigl accepts no responsibility for any such changes. All media enhanced books are regularly monitored to update addresses and sites in a timely manner. Contact AV² by Weigl at 1-866-649-3445 or av2books@weigl.com with any questions, comments, or feedback.